PRESENT TENSE

poems

Neil Silberblatt

PublishAmerica
Baltimore

© 2013 by Neil Silberblatt.
All rights reserved. No part of this book may be reproduced, stored in a retrieval system or transmitted in any form or by any means without the prior written permission of the publishers, except by a reviewer who may quote brief passages in a review to be printed in a newspaper, magazine or journal.

First printing

PublishAmerica has allowed this work to remain exactly as the author intended, verbatim, without editorial input.

Softcover 9781627728812
PUBLISHED BY PUBLISHAMERICA, LLLP
www.publishamerica.com
Baltimore

Printed in the United States of America

*to all the poets, writers & musicians who have shared their
words, voices & talents at our
Voices of Poetry events –
with admiration, respect & gratitude*

Several of the poems in this collection were previously published.

After the Tempest was published in *Verse Wisconsin* (October 2012).

Madison Avenue was selected by *Hennen's Observer* as the Grand Prize Winner for its Open Community Poetry Contest (July 1 - September 30, 2012), and was nominated for a *Pushcart Prize*.

Stand Your Ground was published in *Verse Wisconsin* (October 2012).

The Stroke was published in *Naugatuck River Review* (August 2013).

CONTENTS

INTRODUCTION xi

Tall Trees and Low Sky 1

After the Tempest 2

Stand Your Ground 4

New York Suite – A Tour in Verse 7

    I. East Village 7

    II. West Village 8

    III. Madison Avenue 10

    IV. Fifth Avenue 12

    V. Fulton Fish Market 13

    VI. The Flower District 15

    VII. Wall Street 16

    VIII. Diamond District 18

    IX. Meatpacking District 21

    X. Number 4 Train (Lexington Avenue Downtown Express) 22

    XI. Central Park (The Carousel) 23

    XII. High Line Park 25

    XIII. The Lady 27

XIV. Harlem (August 1958) 29

XV. Harlem (for Sylvia) 33

XVI. Upper West Side 34

The Evening News 37

The Beauty Pageant 39

Time, the Great Healer (for S.) 41

Peonies 42

Conrad 44

The Matador 46

A Sunday Service (at the Sikh Temple) 49

Fine & Mellow (for Billie) 50

A Linguist's Dilemma 51

One Small Step 52

Radiographic Representation of Her Lady Parts 54

Labor 56

A Bowl of Red (for Vernon) 58

Licking for Bobby 59

The Potato Eaters 61

The Slave Ship 63

Targeted Killing	65
The Second Time 11/06/2012	67
Redemption	69
Chana	70
Aisle 14	72
411 Elm	73
Wonder (for Zoe)	75
If he	76
Stations of the Cross	77
That Red Stuff	79
My Month	80
Leftovers (for Annie)	81
The Long Courtship & Short Marriage of Ethel & Ernie	82
And Now, For My Next Trick	83
The Stroke	85
The Fourth Day	86
The Wardrobe	88
Hah Lachma	89
A Song for Goldberg	91

By Your Leave 92

The Evangelist 93

Wachet Auf 95

Time Out (for Pablo) 96

Marathon 98

Strawberries 100

Wisdom's Gate 101

Memorial Day (2012) 102

Memorial Day (2013) 104

Acknowledgments 105

Biography 107

INTRODUCTION

This is my second published collection of poems. In the year since the first collection (*So Far, So Good*) was published, I have written much; tried to write more; read my work at various events; and organized events for other poets to read their work. All are satisfying in equal measure. All present their own unique set of challenges, waiting to be overcome. I hope to continue doing all.

Many of the poems in this collection were inspired by the city of my birth, childhood, adolescence and a good chunk of my adulthood. Despite the title *New York Suite*, the poems are not meant to offer a tour of streets, avenues, buildings or neighborhoods of the isle of Manhattan. Instead, they offer a tour of memory – which is far more lasting and less prone to graffiti. The poems are not meant as documentary accounts. Thus, the man who invited me to pray with him in a "mitzvah mobile" in *Diamond District* existed; but he did not accost me in the manner I describe. The woman depicted in *Madison Avenue* – who set up a display of handbags on the corner of 78th Street - also existed; but I cannot be sure if she is from Senegal and she was not eating a plum when I saw and spoke with her. Sadly, the incident described in *Fifth Avenue* did take place; but my response at the time was not as poetic as I might have wished. Some of the poems in that "group" do not describe buildings or neighborhoods at all. *The Lady,* for example, is about one of the many homeless women in the City, who still doubtless stands with her hand outstretched.

Several of the poems in this collection (*After the Tempest, A Sunday Service, That Red Stuff, And Now, For My Next Trick, The Fourth Day* and *Hah Lachma*) deal with spiritual or religious issues. That is because – for most of my life, starting with my elementary education in a Jewish day school – I have wrestled with issues of faith. I am still wrestling. No victor has been declared as of yet.

Many of these poems (*Stand Your Ground, A Sunday Service, A Linguist's Dilemma, Licking for Bobby, The Second Time, Marathon*) deal with political issues or what used to be referred to as "current events" – from President Kennedy's assassination (*411 Elm*) to the assassination of suspected terrorists (*Targeted Killing*). There is good reason for that. Poets, like plumbers, live and work in the real world and are shaped by events in it. If I watch the news and hear of the massacre of children in a village in Syria, I have two choices: I can scream or I can write (*The Evening News*). In that case, the poem is my scream.

I have been told, by a former beloved English teacher and by several readers and listeners, that I am a story-teller in verse. I consider that high praise, since I have always regarded story-telling as an essential component of good writing (in fiction, poetry or memoir) – but I am not entirely sure if it is well-deserved. That is for you, the reader of these words, to decide.

Some people who "inspired" certain of these poems merit special mention. *A Bowl of Red* is in memory of Vernon Cherry, a firefighter in Brooklyn and friend lost – after he and his crew raced into the still-burning World Trade Center – on September 11, 2001. *Harlem (for Sylvia)* is for Sylvia Woods, the owner of the restaurant on Lenox Avenue which still bears her name and so much else of her. *Fine & Mellow* is in loving tribute to Billie Holiday and her lead tenor sax man Lester "Pres" Young. *A Linguist's Dilemma* is in less-than-loving tribute to Rep. Todd Akin. *One Small Step* is my poetic eulogy to Neil Armstrong, one of the icons of my youth. *If he* is my musing on what could have led a 20-year old man to massacre school children and teachers in Newtown, Connecticut. *Leftovers* is my homage to Annie Orr, who selflessly dedicated many years of her life to helping the poor and homeless in Danbury. On a personal note, *Strawberries* is for a woman loved and lost to cancer; *Wonder* is for my daughter Zoe; *Chana* (her original name, before it was Anglicized to Anita) is for my mother; and *Tall Trees and Low Sky* and *The Stroke* are for my late father – with considerable love for all.

Neil Silberblatt
July 2013

PRESENT TENSE

poems

Tall Trees and Low Sky

What did Daedelus say to his son
as he applied wax to his feathered wings?
Did he offer to take the young man's place,
before Icarus
                              leaping
became a study in epaulement
over the tall trees, into the low sky?

What did Abraham say to his infant son Ishmael,
as he put him to bed the night before
he banished him to starve in the wilderness
among the tall trees, under the low sky?

What did Isaac say to his father,
as he beheld the axe and kindling
and no goat
as they approached the altar
hidden by the tall trees, against the low sky?

What did Daedelus say to his wife
when he returned home that spring evening,
without his son,
having tearfully gathered the feathers raining
from the low sky onto the tall trees?

And what shall I say to you
now that you're gone
when words will never
bridge the chasm
between trees and sky?

March 7, 2012 (New York Daily News) - Pat Robertson believes the victims of the tornadoes that swept through the nation brought the death and devastation upon themselves by not praying enough.

"God didn't send the tornadoes," the ... evangelist said .... "God set up a world in which certain currents interfere and interact with other currents. If enough people were praying, He would intervene."

After the Tempest

These shards of wood
    are the roof of our home,
        which His finger flicked away,
            along with our infant daughter
                asleep in her crib,
            like so much lint
    plucked from
a dishcloth.

This twisted frame
    is our bed,
        which He blew
           across fields and villages
              and cities,
        until it came to rest
    among startled cows
  who, to their consternation,
had been left to graze by the highway.
He does this every so often
this El Maleh Rachamim[1]
    in His infinite jest

---

[1] Hebrew for "God, full of compassion". The opening words in a Jewish memorial prayer recited at a gravesite and upon the observance of the anniversary of a loved one's death.

      His careless cruelty
a tsunami here
a plague there,
causing the rivers to swell
or bleed,
causing the winds and widows to howl,
to show us He can
  to mock our absurd impermanence
   to avenge His son, perhaps
    to test our faith
     to start anew when He cannot
      find the ten righteous souls
who are now interred
in the Lower 9th Ward.

And these damp scraps of cloth
      are our children
           their bodies
                    lost in waves
          like Pharaoh's army,
       their lives poured out
     like so many grains of salt
that were once not so long ago
Lot's wife.

"American history is longer, larger, more various, more beautiful, and more terrible than anything anyone has ever said about it."
James Baldwin

Stand Your Ground

Stand your ground
like a tree that's planted by the water,
near the banks of the North Canadian River
this clear day in May,
as you jostle with others
for a good spot
to take pictures
of Laura and
her 15 year old boy Lawrence[2]
hanging from the bridge
like strange fruit.

Stand your ground
by the large sycamore tree near City Hall in Waco
on another day in May,
as 17 year old Jesse,[3]
his body muscled
from hauling bales of hay
now naked and beaten,
baptized in coal oil,

---

[2] Laura Nelson was raped; she and her 15-year old son Lawrence were then hanged from a bridge over the North Canadian River on May 25, 1911. Hundreds of sightseers gathered on the bridge the following morning, and photographs of the hanging bodies were sold as postcards.

[3] Jesse Washington was a 17-year old farmhand who was tortured and lynched on May 15, 1916 after he was found guilty in a one-hour long trial for the rape and murder of a wealthy 53-year-old white woman. Although Jesse signed a confession, he was by all accounts illiterate.

hoisted like a flag
by his neck, and
lowered into the fire,
as the flames lick his skin
and his wordless screams fill the
smoke-filled spring sky.

Stand your ground
near the noisy fairgrounds by the silent railyard
as young Henry[4]
is placed upon a scaffold,
ten feet high,
and his body is caressed
by red hot iron brands
as kerosene is poured upon him,
and set alight,
as little ones eat fried dough
and wave banners.

Stand your ground
along an asphalt road this dark night in June,
as James,[5] his feet bound -
like a latter-day Saint Sebastian -
is driven across the back roads of Jasper
greeting every rock, every stone

---

4   *17-year old Henry Smith was tortured and murdered at a public, heavily attended lynching on February 1, 1893 at the Paris Fairgrounds in Paris, Texas. Six days later, Henry's stepson, William Butler, was also lynched due to suspicion that he had known, and not divulged, the whereabouts of Henry Smith after he had fled.*
5   *James Byrd, Jr. was murdered by three white men in Jasper, Texas on June 7, 1998, when he was dragged behind a pick-up truck with a heavy logging chain wrapped around his ankles. Byrd was pulled along for about three miles as the truck swerved from side to side. Byrd - who reportedly remained conscious throughout most of the ordeal - was killed when his body hit the edge of a culvert, severing his right arm and head.*

until his body
gives out.

Stand your ground
for this child, his skin
the color of
the soil of those river banks
the bark of that sycamore
the lumber of that kerosene-soaked scaffold
the dirt of that Jasper road
has not been the first
who has been laid low
for no reason.

Stand your ground
though it quakes
though it opens beneath you
though it threatens to swallow you whole.

Stand your ground,
like a tree that's planted by the water;
you shall not,
no, you shall not be moved.

New York Suite – A Tour in Verse

I.   East Village

And here is where I was taken
trembling, at eight days
for a ritual
linking me with a race
for which I had never trained.

And here is where my father was taken
trembling, at sixty years
the left side of his face
contorted
as he struggled to form the words
"not without my son".

And here is where I was taught
to believe and fear,
and learned instead
to doubt and disdain.

And here is where
we laughed and swung so high
on playground swings
or woodwinds,
the air lifting our feet
or our notes,
before we came crashing
back to earth.

No photos please; these places
no longer exist.
They are mere stops
in a Baedeker of memory.

II.   West Village

If you go to the narrow streets
of the West Village
past the incongruous intersection
of 4th and 11th Streets,
do not walk.
Wander.
Stroll.
Meander.
Better yet,
get lost.

For then you may chance upon
the slender house where
Edna St. Vincent Millay wrote her slender verse,
or the house on Patchin Place where
Edward Estlin became e.e.,
railed against "kikes"
and dreamt in lower case.

Do not walk with a destination in mind,
for then you might miss the White Horse
where Dylan Thomas raged, raged
against the dying of his light,
or where John Reed and Emma Goldman
simply raged.

These narrow streets
still hold the memories of
their footsteps,
the echoes of
their fingers on typewriters,
      that ancient tool,
the sound of their laughter.

But, if you walk
through The Village
too quickly,
you will miss these echoes.
So, by all means,
get lost.

III.   Madison Avenue

At the Viand Coffee Shop
on Madison Avenue
    which must not be confused
    with the Viand on East 86th
    or the Viand on Broadway
come the young ladies fresh from
their visit to the Met
or, if they dare, the Whitney
    because one can only
    take so many Rothkos
    or Van Goghs
    in a morning
wearing their
dazzling tennis whites
which have never seen,
and will never see,
a ground stroke
as they pick apart their salads
and each other.

Enter the ladies bearing handbags
with names like children,
the real thing of course,
no knock offs here
as they survey
the dieter's special
and eye the desserts
cordoned off behind the counter.
Their conversations hushed
as they spread butter
and gossip.

Two blocks away
from the Viand Coffee Shop
on Madison Avenue
      which must not be confused
      with the Viand on East 86th
      or the Viand on Broadway
stands a refugee
from Senegal
as black as the plum into which she bites,
its juices dripping down the side of her hand
as she hurriedly sets up
her display of handbags
on the street-corner.

She is
real;
the plum is
real;
the bags –
      as she will quietly tell you
           in her rich Senegalese accent,
                with her breath scented by plum -
are beautiful,
but fake.

IV.   Fifth Avenue

We walked
arm in arm
that summer evening
down Fifth Avenue
oblivious to the rain
and history.

As we walked
toward the Park,
a well-dressed man
looked at us disapprovingly
and then his words came
like a dagger
sotto voce
"Nigger Lover."

Shaking with rage,
I wanted to rip
the hateful words
from his throat
and his throat from his body.

Instead, I smiled at our assailant
and said "You bet,"
and kissed you full on the lips
in front of Tiffany's
and god.

V.   Fulton Fish Market

Oddly, the first thing you noticed
was not the smell.
Like dirt at a freshly dug grave,
it was not the *smell* you noticed.

No, the first thing you noticed
as you came around the corner of South Street
and approached the fishmarket
at 4 a.m. –
when the city's towers were still dark,
and the FDR drive vacant,
and even the subways asleep,
was the noise.

What noise, you ask.
Shouts, screams of all manner of seafood
cut the air
in accents as varied as the fish.
Scallops shouted in Portugese.
Tilapia or monkfish screamed in Italian.
Salmon and tuna grunted in Japanese -
a maritime tower of babel.

As men with muscles in their cheekbones
and tendons in their eyebrows
hauled these creatures
from the ocean onto trucks.

There, swordfish -
dwarfed only by the ocean.
There, giant squid -
their inky writing days behind them.

There, giant octopus -
with its long legs
········or were they arms
idling on packets of ice.

These magnificent creatures
and their captors
once ruled the Atlantic.

Now, they
and the fishmarket
sleep with the fishes.

VI.   The Flower District

In the morning,
no, that is not quite right,
for it is still dark outside
forests, groves, meadows, fields of flowers,
rows of boxwoods
descend upon the City
quietly
stealthily
in trucks.

Like undocumented workers,
illegal aliens,
they congregate,
crammed unwillingly into the backs of vans,
hiding
waiting
in the dark
until the proper moment
when they can breathe free
and set down roots.

Behold, now comes
in a U-Haul with squeaking axles
as it double parks illegally
on 6th Avenue
Great Birnam Wood to midtown Manhattan.

VII. Wall Street

Unlike the streets which run
                    p a r a l l e l
or   p
        e
        r
        pendicular
such as Cedar and Pine
        cobblestoned tributes to the trees
        that once stood here
or Fulton
        which celebrates great men and
        great deeds
or Maiden
        which evokes images of
        fair women
or Bowling Green
        which stirs memories of
        children's games
this street
        commemorates neither tree
        nor man
        nor good deed
        nor games.

No, this street was named after
something far more modest:
a wall,
a stockade really,
but Stockade Street would not have the
same ring to it.

Twelve feet high, built and reinforced
by the Dutch settlers

      led by their governor, Peter Stuyvesant,
      the great man who seized the few possessions
      of the resident Jews, ordered them sold,
      and – when that did not satisfy –
      sought permission to expel the infidels from
       this island
with the aid of African slaves,
      their names lost to history,
      who were doubtless
      glad for the opportunity
      to build their masters' fortress
to keep out and subdue the Indians
      who were here when the Dutch were
      still asleep in Amsterdam.

The Dutch are now gone.
The Indians are gone.
The slaves are gone.
The wall too is gone.

Nevertheless,
it is a fitting name
for this street.

VIII. Diamond District

"Meesteh. Ay, Meesteh".
He stands there rooted
on the corner of 47th and 5th
a stone's throw and worlds away
from St. Patrick's and Saks
in this blistering heat
dressed defiantly
in the garb of oppression
long black coat
and fur-trimmed hat,
missing only the yellow star.

*"Meesteh,
Iz vuz a Yid?"*[6]
he loudly inquires of chosen passersby
most of whom do just that -
>   except he pronounces it
>   "yeed", as in creed -
speaking in the language of ghosts,
the lexicon of the dead.

He waits for a reciprocal glance
of recognition,
for if one understands the question
one has already answered it.

He does not pose this question to those
dressed like him,
as they make their way to
their jewelry counters,
sizing gems

---

[6]   *Yiddish or German for "Are you a Jew?"*

carrying fortunes in satchels
ready for the next pogrom.
Their souls are already secure.

No, he poses this question to those
a generation removed
from the survivors of the ovens,
or the children of the lucky ones
who came before the troubles began.

He catches my eye,
as I try like mad to avoid his
"*Meesteh, Iz vuz a Yid?,*" he asks,
his spittle caught in his straggly beard
along with yesterday's egg salad sandwich
which hides there
like Moses in the bulrushes.

I do not respond.
What is there to say?
He knows the answer.
Yes, *ich bin eine Yid*[7]
the descendant of those
like him, the second or third cousin of
an 18-year old fresh from *cheder*[8]
who had his skull smashed
for the sin of believing in a merciful god.

I continue on my way,
spurning his invitation to *daven*[9] in an R.V.

---

7   *Yiddish or German for "I am a Jew".*

8   *Hebrew or Yiddish for religious school.*

9   *Hebrew or Yiddish for pray or worship.*

re-christened as a "*mitzvah*[10] mobile",
making a right turn toward 47th and Sixth,
as he continues to fish for tarnished souls
in this diamond district,
rooted on the corner
of Vilnius and 5th.

---

10 *Hebrew or Yiddish for commandment or good deed.*

IX.   Meatpacking District

Two days ago, this one here
stripped bare with her marbled flesh
hanging with her mates
along 14th Street
amidst men with blood-stained aprons
and ill intent
was chewing grass in a pen
by the stockyards,
happily ignorant of her fate.

Two years ago, this one here
stripped almost bare with her marbled flesh
hanging with her mates
along 14th Street
after they have hosed down the streets
amidst men with suits
and ill intent
was smoking grass in a home
by the stockyards
happily ignorant of her fate.

This meat on the hoof
shares the same cobblestoned street
with meat on the heel,
their flesh satisfying the appetites of man,
neither imagining
they will be devoured.

X. Number 4 Train (Lexington Avenue Downtown Express)

Crammed in like sardines
and so we were
pressed against doors
praying they would not open,
our bodies closer than lovers
our eyes focused on
ads for smooth(er) skin
as we avoided
the stranger's touch
or glance.

And yet,
a sardine
would never have offered his seat
to the dark-haired beauty
clutching her sleeping newborn
to her chest
with one hand
as she held her high school bag
in the other
and silently mouthed the words

"thank you".

XI.   Central Park (The Carousel)

The hair on her mane and tail
was darker
       the color of Crayola's Burnt Sienna
and less matted
when I rode her
across the Alps with Hannibal, slaying Huns
or bareback
shooting at marauding Indians
       when Indians still marauded
       before dinner
       before we knew better
or across the quiet English countryside
       quiet except for the distant
       but unmistakable
       song without lyrics of the beckoning
       Mister Softee truck.

She knew my touch
no matter how many others rode her
responding to my every command
stooping slightly to allow me
to mount her
rising again after
my feet were firmly in her stirrups
and I held her reins
and her nostrils flared
breathing for me alone.

And how she moved –
silently
swiftly
racing past avenues
taxis

Sabrett carts,
across continents and oceans,
if my voice so commanded
always to the same tune
which we both knew
by heart.

Now, she and I
are both closed for needed repairs
and hope to reopen soon.

XII. High Line Park

Do rails hold thoughts of rust
when they cease to carry freight
and our bones have turned to dust
and conductors are all late?

Do weeds hold dreams of flowers
when they strive to find the air
through the passing of the hours
and the tenements' cold glare?

The trains no longer ride through here
their ghosts still roam the yards
the call of trainmen linger near
as their specters play at cards.

Now, this terminus is breathed anew
and children's laughs delight
and lilacs bloom where weeds once grew
and moss has conquered blight.

On this line where trains once roared
their iron ghosts now creak
Instead, one sees a grassy floor
and can hear the horses speak.

From the High Line
by Susan Grisell
(reprinted with permission of the artist)

XIII. The Lady

The freezing wind blows off the water
down Broadway
finding every gap in her tattered dress
every exposed bit of skin
erasing even the memory
of warmth.

She stands there
buffeted by the winds
utterly alone
in this city of millions.
No roof over her head.
No place to rest it either.
Standing with her hand outstretched,
wearing sandals,
which cannot possibly keep her feet warm.

Though thousands pass by,
none looks her in the eye.
None comes to her aid.
None ventures close.

Still – despite her age –
her face is of a young woman.
One can see that
in her youth
she was a beauty.

Must have turned heads
that long neck
those eyes
that slender build.

Oh yes, she once was quite the beauty,
but that was ages ago.
And what she has endured -
the name calling
> wop
> dago
> yid
> mick
> spic
> greaseball
> wetback
> guinea.

She's been called that
and worse
which cuts like the ocean air,
though she will never admit it.

She just stands there
with that damned torch,
waiting for the next bunch
of blessed fools
yearning to breathe free.

XIV. Harlem (August 1958)

It was a hot day.
The City in August -
way too damn hot to be posing in
suits and ties.
But that's what we wore that Sunday
in front of a tenement on 126th near Fifth.
Not that Fifth,
this aint no Tiffany neighborhood.

10 a.m. – A.M.!
for a picture for some gentleman's magazine
they didn't sell at newstands in Harlem
even though we was gentlemen.

10 a.m. - hell, that's no time to be awake
not for a jazz man.
But we all showed up –
except for Marian's boy
who couldn't get out of bed -
on time too, or nearly.

Brownstone he called it. Yeah, right.
The only thing brown that day
was the color of my sweat
and the stains on my armpits.

Count, he got tired of standing
so he pulled up some curb
with kids who had no idea
who we were.

Lester was there too,
Pres - that's what Billie called him
and it stuck.
He'd be gone five months later,
just a hair under 50.
But that Sunday morning,
he was there in that porkpie.

Speaking of porkpie,
Mingus came too
looking kinda' ticked off,
10 a.m. – like I said
no time to be awake
but not so that he would miss standing
on that stoop
on that Sunday.

Monk, Dizzy - what a clown
making his usual face
trying to crack us up
Krupa, even Coleman
we was all there
waiting for that man
from that gentleman's magazine
they didn't sell up in Harlem
waiting for him to take that damn picture
so we gentlemen could take our damn ties off
and jam
or go back to bed.

The camera boy
yelled for us to smile.
And we did,
except Mingus
who still looked kinda' ticked off.

Then, the shutter clicked
the ground shifted
swallowed us all
chewed us up
spit us out.

Later, Fidel would show up in Harlem
just to rub Ike's nose in it.
Malcolm would get it;
then Martin.
Then, these streets bled and burned
even 126th near Fifth
as men in blue too scared
to come north of 116th
urged us to
"stay calm".
Still, man, that was a time.

We got together last week for another shoot
waiting for Sonny, Benny and Marian
to show up.

They'll be here.
They're just running late.
Smile, the man said.
And we did,
even Mingus.[11]

---

11 *On Sunday, August 12, 1958 at 10:00 a.m., Art Kane -- a freelance photographer for Esquire magazine -- took a photo of 57 jazz musicians gathered in front of 17 East 126th Street in New York City.*

The list of musicians who posed for that photo – which includes Count Basie, Lester Young, Gene Krupa, Dizzy Gillespie, Coleman Hawkins, Thelonious Monk and Charles Mingus (who can be seen scowling in the photo) – reads like a who's who of jazz. Of the group who gathered that morning, only three remain: Sonny Rollins, Benny Golson and Marian McPartland.

XV. Harlem (for Sylvia)

She was one of a breed of settlers
who came to these hallowed streets
from the fields of Memphis
and the slaughterhouses of Chicago
just for a taste.

She welcomed all
not with open arms -
since open arms are empty
or with words
which are emptier still –
but with heaving arms and sweating face
bearing bounty on groaning platters
urging just a taste.

If she could tear herself away
from the steam of that kitchen
long enough
to hear these words,
she would rebuke the mourners
her hands akimbo on her ample hips.

"Don't just say you love me.
Suck on my ribs."

XVI. Upper West Side

In the shadow of the mighty Apthorp
with her cloistered courtyard,
six blocks from the Ansonia with her ample walls
home to the Bambino and Stravinsky
>	one wonders if they ever met in the elevator
>	and compared notes or
>	scores,
overlooked by the twin towers of the San Remo,
before another twin towers claimed the skyline,
  for a time
before the War, before the Flood
before buildings had need of addresses
>	when they had names, other than a
>	real estate developer's vainglorious son,
stands the old man, in worn raincoat, though
>	it is not raining
>	and is not expected to
feeding the pigeons who gather for him at the apex
of 79th and Broadway.

Scattering bread crumbs from boundless pockets,
he yells at the occasional squirrel who ventures
  too close.
"Schnorrer! Chazer!", chasing away these
  interlopers who, by now,
know the routine and flee, but only
after they have scored some bread.

With untraceable accent, he coos to his winged patrons
who return the favor
while they perch on arms and back,
as he mimics a scarecrow
and they conduct an avian stop and frisk.

Having emptied his pockets of treasure,
he clutches his paper with undone crossword
and returns to his pre-war flat
where he will refill his pre-war pockets
and birds will gather outside his pre-war window
and remind him to return
to their corner.

Windy Day at the Met
by Susan Grisell
(reprinted with permission of the artist)

The Evening News

The man on my screen,
with his blue silk tie
and perfect hair,
tells me that 49 children were
slaughtered today
in a village which
I have never heard of,
and which
I cannot find on a map,
but which
is now enshrined with other villages
famous for mass graves
filled with small coffins.

He shares this information
with the same
flat measured speech
with which
he shares
the long-term weather forecast.
49 children slaughtered
and chance of
thunderstorms.

This will not do.
No, this will not do at all.

He needs to rend his clothing,
to tear at that nice tie,
to pull at that perfect hair.
He needs to scream
or, at least, weep.
Yes, weeping would do nicely
before he shuffles his papers
and cuts to commercial.

Such words -
children slaughtered -
should scorch the tongue,
assault the ear.
Even god waited until
Pharaoh had tried his patience
nine times
before resorting to that.

Such news should be screamed
or, at least, cried out
through tears
as Jonah screamed his warning of god's fury
to the people of Nineveh,
which is just down the road
from Houla.

Haifa, Israel (AP) – June 29, 2012 – "Grinning and waving, 14 women who survived the horrors of World War II paraded Thursday in an unusual pageant, vying for the honor of being crowned ... [the] first 'Miss Holocaust Survivor.'"

The Beauty Pageant

Here she is.
Isn't she lovely?
Look at that slender figure,
that gaunt smile
and vacant stare.
And that striped gown
not quite a gown exactly -
more like pajamas –
which hangs from her bones
like a shroud.
But she wears it so well,
doesn't she?

As she walks down the runway,
pay note to her posture
still hobbled by disease.
Scurvy perhaps?
Rickets?
Possibly scoliosis,
hard to say.
Some Vitamin D deficiency, certainly.
Naturally, the beatings did not help.
Nevertheless, she walks beautifully.
Wouldn't you agree?

And that smile,
that dazzling smile.
If only, she had more of her own teeth.

The gold fillings, of course,
were removed –
gold being so valuable.
You understand.
But the smile still captures
her joie d'vivre.

No, she is unquestionably
a true winner -
really, no contest.

Please join me in
welcoming the new
Miss Therezinstadt.
*Yisgodal, v'yiskaddash
shemay rabbah.*[12]

Light a candle for her
on the way out,
would you.

---

12 *Hebrew for "May His name be celebrated and glorified." The opening words of the "Kaddish", commonly known as the mourner's prayer.*

Time, the Great Healer (for S.)

In time,
that great healer
which turns mountains to sand
and bones to ash,
I will forget all.
I will forget
the taste of your lips
the echo of your laugh
the scent of your breasts
the resonance of your words
the sweetness of your touch.

In time,
my arms will cease to move,
or to ache
from the lack of you.

In time,
my eyes will close or
forget your smile
when you smiled
with your eyes closed.

In time, I will do all this
and more.
When they scatter dirt over me,
I will start
to try.

Peonies

He finds her in the garden
hidden.
She spears him with a glance so brief
it is gone before …

She is closed now.
Through January's snow and April's rain,
she has stood by
patiently waiting
enduring
for this moment.

He brings her inside looking at her
with a look that
silently
speaks volumes.

Now, at last, she is with him,
but never his.

Safe inside,
he buries his face among her petals
breathing in her scent
filling every pore
as his breath warms her
deeply.

Observing the petals
as Galileo observed the universe
awed
humbled.

At last, when his courage mounts
he touches them
careful not to open them
more than
they wish to be opened.

And they respond
releasing their cloistered embrace -
a strand of horse's hair
coaxed to play Bach,
so it is with her
and him.

With his breath still inside her
and his touch still felt
she opens
saying
behold me
for this moment,
I am beauty.

Conrad

Forever sandwiched between his wife
    who died too young
    her family name lost
    identified by the stone cutter
    only as "wife of Conrad"
and the daughter
    who lived to see old age
    and never married
    or bore child
he rests.

Reposing between these two women
on this grassy hill –
disappointment on either side.
The pain of loss,
emptiness of marital bed,
lack of generations to carry on,
indignity of an early death
exceeded only
by the misspelling of his first name
for all eternity.

Did his daughter not notice
the cutter's error?
Was this her parting slight,
or could she not bear
the grief
or cost of correction?
The lichen-covered slab
offers no details
beyond the dates of arrival and departure
of the less-than-beloved
Coonrad.

When it is my turn to be planted,
skip the benedictions.
Just see that my name is
spelled wright.

The Matador

Relax a moment.
I can see you are tired.

I meant to ask
about the cape.
Why the cape?

Did you think I would not notice you
in your splendid finery
once you led me
into this stadium,
this abbatoir
with spectators.
Did you think that I would lose interest
once you
slid the sword
into my side.

Really, no need for a cape.
If I could find a blade of grass
in a barren field,
I would find you
as easily
as your sword found
the space between
my ribs.

And why the *third* sword?
I can understand the first two -
to get my attention,
to whet my appetite
for revenge.
But the third?
But you are tired,
I see.

The chase round the ring
in this heat
has exhausted you.
Perhaps that last thrust
of the steel
into my shoulder blades
     as the gentlemen cheered,
     the ladies screamed,
     and the boys hawked cerveza
awakened an old injury
pierced some dormant conscience.

Rest awhile here.
Regain your strength.
I can wait.

Next time,
I bring the cape.

48

A Sunday Service (at the Sikh Temple)

Had there been a baptismal font,
a shallow pool of water,
bearing the fingerprints of parishioners,
would that have
stayed his hand?

Would a stained glass or marble
depiction of a madonna
weeping over the body of her son
have caused him to
pause
just a moment
before opening fire?

Perhaps, some words
muttered responsively
in Latin
       if only he had heard Latin
might have made him
realize that this was not
a battlefield
and these
were not combatants.

But this was a god,
and these were a people,
he did not know.

So much
can depend upon
a shallow pool
of water.

Fine & Mellow (for Billie)

Her right eyebrow
stenciled
acting independently
of its mate.

Her right eyebrow
arching slowly skyward
      on the fourth bar
      of Fine & Mellow
      as Pres entered
a child reaching for that container
on the highest shelf
certain of its sweet contents

Her right eyebrow
pulled upwards by no
muscular contraction
or cigarette smoke,
though there was plenty
in that studio
with all those guys afire.

Her right eyebrow
responding to measures
blown by Pres
through pressed lips.

Her right eyebrow
soaring, laughing
silencing all question
as to what he was to her
or she to him.

St. Louis, Missouri – August 19, 2012 -- "If it's a legitimate rape, the female body has ways to try to shut the whole thing down." Interview of Rep. Todd Akin (Republican candidate for Senate) on KTVI-TV.

A Linguist's Dilemma

These two words
"legitimate rape"
do not belong conjoined.
Rape needs no adjective.
It craves no first name.

It desires only
time
to forget
to purge the image
from her body
her mind
as if such a thing were possible.
It begs for warm water
and hard-bristled brush
to scrub the stain and stench
of his body
from hers.

These words
are ill-matched,
the first doing brutal injustice to the other
by its proximity
as much as assailant
and victim.

No, this simple man
could not have meant this as adjective.
He must have meant it
in its ancient use –
as verb.

One Small Step

It was never the same
afterwards.
He had been warned about
the shock of re-entry –
how alien this world would seem,
how barren.

Tests were conducted on
the effects of prolonged weightlessness.
Blood was taken -
before
after.
No tests, however, on the more disastrous
effects of
prolonged gravity,
which always proves fatal.

When he returned
after leaving his heel print
on that surface
on our imagination
they found no lasting impact.
The skin retained its elasticity.
The organs returned to their pre-orbital positions.
The blood resumed flowing
only less easily.
Though, he could not blame that
on the moon.

Later, when he slowly descended
his steps
carefully positioning
each foot
on each rung
to retrieve the morning paper,
the surface did not show the contours of his shoes.

At night, in a cloudless sky,
he would sometimes glance at her
like accidentally coming across a photo of a lover
now gone.

He could never return to her,
comforted only by the sure knowledge that,
on a summer's night,
he had left his mark
on her
and on us.

Radiographic Representation of Her Lady Parts

The x-ray glasses which he ordered
from the back pages of comic books
next to ads which showed a weakling
metamorphosed
after sand and humiliation
were hurled into his face
in equal measure
which promised to allow him
to see past women's clothing
      never men's
did not work as advertised
on either gender.

He abandoned those glasses
long ago.

Now, he stood by the light box
which worked so much better
with its slides of forms
barely discernible as human,
cross-sectioned accounts of
her form.

Examining the slides, he beheld all.
Here, her smooth breasts
without false modesty.
He could trace the translucent arc of her back,
following it as Stanley followed the Nile,
searching for its source.
There, the small folds of flesh
or their ghostly memory.

He scanned all
in her fluorescent splendor,
searching for disease or imperfection.

He surveyed past
skin
cartillage
muscle
to
organ
bone.

Like the glasses
which did not work as advertised
these slides ultimately revealed
all,
and nothing,
of her beauty.

Labor

In pain shall you bring forth children,[13]
and by the sweat of your brow
shall you make your bread
until you return to dust[14]…

Labor - it was His punishment
for their transgression,
their flouting of His very first commandment,
the first example of many
of His wrath.

The boy had been taught these lessons
on Sundays – which came with
endless warnings of flames below
with the smell of pitch and heat
so oppressive
that one's lungs collapsed.
He knew that smell and that heat.

The boy remembered these lessons
as he squeezed his twelve-year old body
into the coal cart,
as he made his descent
to coax the anthracite with tiny hands.

---

13 *Genesis 3:16.*

14 *Genesis 3:19.*

As he recalled his father
whose lungs had collapsed
and who had returned to dust,
the boy wondered –
what sin had he committed in his twelve years
to incur His wrath.

A Bowl of Red (for Vernon)

You spoke that day of heat,
the way the Inuit speak of snow
with reverence and fear,
not in celsius or fahrenheit,
but in scoville units.

A good bowl of red demands cayenne
you insisted, and lots of it
as though a bowl of red has ever demanded anything
but a cold glass with a nice foam.

We debated as to whether red or white - or any -
beans should be used, and which peppers,
as though debating matters of great import,
not recalling which side I advanced in this great debate
other more pressing matters having arisen
or fallen.

You spoke of fire,
as a man well acquainted with heat
not on the skin, but on the tongue.
As it turns out, you were scared of neither.

That morning, after you raced inside the melting towers,
another heat embraced you
kissing you full on the mouth.

In truth, a bowl of red can make do without cayenne
or beans or peppers.
It demands only a cook with a taste for fire,
and will wait patiently on the stove until he returns.

Licking for Bobby

One envelope tastes so much like another
to a twelve year old tongue,
with reserves of saliva drained
then replenished
with that residual taste of …
was it spearmint?

Stacks of envelopes waiting to be kissed
by my virgin lips, but only after
they were filled with flyers
exhorting the recipients to
> give a damn
> be part of the solution,
> not the problem
> feed the hungry
> clothe the naked
> end the war
> quickly,
> before my elder brother,
> like his,
> could be killed.

On each flyer, a black and white photo of the
junior senator from New York
emerging from the roof of a car
leaning towards the cheering throngs
pounding the flesh
tempting fate
squinting, his toothy grin and outstretched hand
and cowlick, tucked neatly
into each envelope
as I would be tucked into bed that evening.

After my tongue was drained,
I returned home to find dinner waiting
convinced that I had
      given a damn
      been part of the solution
      helped feed the poor
      clothe the naked
      end the war
            which would last another five years
a delusion which went down well with
meatloaf,
mashed potatoes
and spearmint.

The Potato Eaters

They have assembled at this strange hour
for, we presume, a meal.
The clock – the only adornment on these walls,
      which more closely resemble a cave -
reads twenty to twelve.
And this is no noonday meal.

And what feast awaits them?
No plates adorn this table,
no cloth, utensils.
No trappings of a meal consumed or
waiting.

There is only coffee
or perhaps cocoa from which no steam rises,
measured out in cups and
a platter of boiled potatoes,
which does not tempt
or satisfy.

As this meal has been stripped of food,
this canvass and their faces have been stripped of color.
No cadmium yellow here, no cobalt.
No vase of sunflowers or Japanese irises offers
respite from the cloistering gray.
Just the dull bluish green of the young man's coat and the
brick red of his pants,
the color of one of Cezanne's apples,
now rotted.

The girl whose back greets us in the foreground
may have served the others.
No chair waits for her.
No food either.
We cannot see her face.
No need.

The Slave Ship

Aloft all hands, strike the top-masts and belay;
Yon angry setting sun and fierce-edged clouds
Declare the Typhon's coming.
Before it sweeps your decks, throw overboard
The dead and dying - ne'er heed their chains
Hope, Hope, fallacious Hope!
Where is thy market now?
    J. M. W. Turner (1812)

If one looks quickly,
passing this painting at the Fine Arts Museum in Boston,
one may see only a spectacular sunset,
  as only Turner could conjure,
harbinger of some biblical storm or maritime disaster and
miss entirely
the sharks and gulls in the lower right foreground
feeding on bloated corpses, which were not quite lifeless
when they were tossed
still chained
into the palegoldenwheat waves.

If one looks quickly,
one may see only the purplebloodred fury of an approaching
storm,
  as only Turner could conjure,
about to wreak its fury on a skeletal ship,
and perhaps feel sorry for her captain and crew,
without knowledge of her worthless,
but valuable, cargo.[15]

---

15 *In 1781, the captain of the slave ship Zong ordered his crew to throw 133 sick or dying slaves overboard so that insurance payments might be collected. The incident reportedly inspired J.M.W. Turner to create this painting.*

You can easily miss such small details
when measured against
a magnificent sunset.

Targeted Killing

"... Mr. Obama has placed himself at the helm of a top secret 'nominations' process to designate terrorists for kill or capture, of which the capture part has become largely theoretical. ... [T]he chart, introducing people whose deaths he might soon be asked to order, underscored just what a moral and legal conundrum this could be."
 Jo Becker & Scott Shane, <u>Secret "Kill List"
 Proves a Test of Obama's Principles</u>,
 NY Times 5/29/2012.

He finally had a bead on him.
At long last, had this tall bearded terrorist in his cross hairs.
Had waited for this moment, to settle debts left open.
No question as to his prey's guilt.
No need to agonize over squeezing the trigger.
 It was never more than a squeeze.

After all, the man in his sights –
who did not sully his hands with the entrails of the innocent
 uttering proclamations of his rectitude,
 invoking the almighty as his ally –
had ordered the deaths of thousands of the soldier's countrymen –
 some merely women and children,
 the feeble of mind or body,
who did nothing more than go about their meaningless daily tasks
or unwittingly choose the wrong side.

This bearded criminal, in his sanctimonious fury,
had given the order to raze a city
bringing devastation and wailing
of a decibel so piercing,
its echoes still resound.

So, once sure of his aim,
the good soldier did not pause to squeeze -
      it was never more than a squeeze -
settling a score
which could never be settled
and, tragically,
missed the second act of "Our American Cousin".

The Second Time
11/06/2012

The first time, we were caught by his newness -
the novelty of his name,
so unlike those on the placemats
of rouged presidents
we gave to our children
to memorize as they played with their food,
a validation that we had progressed beyond such
silly things
        as skin color
        or names,
expiation for a time when
such things mattered.

The first time, we prided ourselves on what we had done
"Look at us," we proclaimed to the world
and to ourselves,
"Only here is this possible.
Forget all that has passed -
those boys in Philadelphia,
        their bodies left to rot;
those children in Sunday school in Birmingham,
        their hair and skin afire.
That is distant past. We are better now."
As though the raising of his right hand and the placing of his left
upon a book
could wipe clean those stains which would make
Lady Macbeth weep.

The first time, we marveled at the strangeness of his parentage,
      half Kansan, half Kenyan,
forgetting a time when such a union was barred
forgetting too our own mongrel races
which clogged the factories and tenements of this island continent.

I prefer the dull routine of the second time,
when his novelty has worn off
and he can take his rightful place
among the rouged presidents;
when we do not comment on his
skin color or parentage
any more than
Hamilton, that bastard
whose blood was eight parts Black.

Redemption

This bottle – alone,
missing its cap and divorced
from its contents –
declares that it cannot be redeemed.
And, perhaps it is so.
It may know more than I;
though open-mouthed, it does not say.

But, if I am not beyond redemption,
then certainly,
there is hope for this bottle.

And, if this bottle
      which caused no harm
      held no evil thought
      and carried nothing but amber liquid
cannot be redeemed,
then truly,
what hope is there for the rest of us?

Chana

Smuggled out in the hull of the S.S. Roma
like illicit cargo
she arrived, seven years old
maybe eight
>she has never been certain and now
>cannot be sure of that
>or much else
with a new hair clip and new name
for the new world.

Her older brother Shimon
>rechristened Seymour
>by some well-intentioned clerk,
>himself nameless
and parents
>Shifra, later Sophie
>and Mendel, who defiantly remained
>Mendel
>but whose last name underwent a trim
>losing consonants as one might lose
>luggage.

Inside Chana's coat,
stuffed between lining and felt,
letters and papers
offering an identity in case she became
separated or lost,
as though she has not already become so.
Now, not quite eight and a half decades later,
she speaks of those days
with greater clarity than more recent days
>or years
and searches my face

as though looking intently at an equation
to which she once knew the answer
asking repeatedly whether I am married,
forgetting the answer
        and the question
asking again
        forgetting again,
struggling to recall
what happened to that little girl
and how she wound up in this place.

Aisle 14

For the moment, they rest here
in the cool mist.

Figs from Lebanon
in close, incestuous embrace;
dates from Syria –
keeping a safe distance from,
and watchful eye on,
thin-skinned Jaffa oranges.

Korean kimchi in forced peaceful co-existence
with Russian beluga
layed out in icy splendor
recalling its days in the bellies of sturgeon
swimming in contested waters.

Olives in military camouflage
harvested from ancient trees in Ramallah,
bulldozed over to make room for settlements,
share space with blood-red pomegranates
culled from collective farms in Judea
fertilized with rockets
imported from Gaza.

This uneasy truce is observed,
as with lions and lambs
who sleep quietly together
until the lion is hungry.

411 Elm

Each of us is all the sums he has not counted: subtract us into the nakedness and night again, and you shall see begin in Crete four thousand years ago the love that ended yesterday in Texas.
	Thomas Wolfe, Look Homeward, Angel

The red brick and arched windows of the
seven-story building at 411 Elm Street
on the northwest corner of Elm and North Houston
> built at the end of the 19th century
> struck, two years later, by lightning,
> nearly burned to the ground
> and rebuilt, two years later,
> in the Romanesque revival style
> so popular then

are not to be found on the postcards and snow-globes
at the airport here.

Nor is the smoothly arched window on the sixth-floor
through which a 24 year old stock room clerk
with a young wife and infant child
hired to help with the holiday rush of filling
textbook orders
watched over a passing motorcade
through a small lens of a long rifle,
or so the commissioners found.

Other structures and other rifles
of which the good people of Texas
are justifiably more proud
vie for attention among the postcards and snow-globes here,
especially the Alamo which,
> despite constant reminders not to,
> in the fall of events,

I have completely forgotten.

Wonder (for Zoe)

She is still too young for the talk
about why this bearded corpulent genie
with his Jolly Green Giant laugh
who, she has been told by friends,
brings bounteous presents
      always the right ones and
      always gift wrapped
will never venture into our home,
though our fireplace is as welcoming as the next.

She is still far too young for the talk
about infants
so tender and mild
and otherwise
how they enter this world
or leave
and perhaps return – though not for us.

She is certainly too young for the talk
about a benevolent god and his chosen people,
offered the choice between
showers that do not clean
and ovens that do not bake.

For now, with melted wax of candles
still on her skin
and the light of those candles
still fresh in her eyes,
as we make our way through snow-bound streets,
she marvels at the glittering lights in all
the other windows
and notes with open-mouthed wonder
how many people celebrate Hanukah
and I do not correct her.

If he

*"...For none can tell to what red Hell
His sightless soul may stray."*
        Oscar Wilde, The Ballad of Reading Gaol

As he formed in the womb,
      if he formed,
was there some insufficiency of
a certain vitamin or mineral
in his mother's diet
which left some cerebral cortex undeveloped
which would have enabled him to perceive children
as something other than paper targets?

As he played,
      if he played,
with wooden blocks and leaden soldiers
holding both at arm's length
as, later, he would hold others
was he allowed to imagine
the effect of real lead?

As he learned,
      if he learned,
the vagaries of language
the certainties of math
was there a lesson left untaught
on the translation of tears
or the multiplication of screams?
Or was this Adam a garden left untended
to grow wild until twisted vines and poisoned
weeds choked out any room for growth
and left their toxins in his soul,
      if he had one.

Stations of the Cross

At 20, he should be on some college quad
broadening his fields,
or vice versa.
Instead, he is asleep in the same
urine and vodka-soaked clothes in which he walked until he
and his shoes gave out
not in that order,
having blown his last paycheck
on smokes and yet more vodka.
"I am not a morning person," he mumbles
as he resists being awakened at 5:30
when the dark is still dark.
The other times of day
will be no more forgiving.

At 54, or 45,
the figure changes according to her mood,
she sets up her twin-size inflatable mattress with
her emphysemic hair blower,
one of her few belongings to accompany her
lone t-shirt and orphaned sweater.
Her hours working at a local hotel are inadequate,
she says,
to afford better.
From the time she arrives
until the moment sleep silences her,
she yammers incessantly on any topic or none
registering complaint upon complaint to all and none
as though filling the space with her noise,
while her blower's breath fills her bed,
will displace a greater absence.

At 58, he more closely resembles the inverse of those numbers
or a scowling scabbed Old Testament prophet
Ezekiel, perhaps
shorn of his beard –
      except on those days or weeks
      when he forgets to shave
if Ezekiel had a two pack a day habit
which he could not afford to keep up
and wore a cheap watch which, like its owner,
had long ceased to work
and whose racking coughs leave even the listener gasping
which this Ezekiel blames on his damned sinuses
because he does not want to, or cannot afford to,
go to the damned hospital
and find out the damned truth.

At 56, he has raised more bottles than children
though he is dry now, or so he says,
and boasts of his 32-year fidelity to his childhood sweetheart
and his beloved Red Sox,
neither of whom can return his affection.
Offering what little he has
to those with less,
cracking the same jokes
over and over
and over
in case the listener has forgotten the punch line
or because he has.

Each of these pilgrims is safe and warm,
for now.
For the night, their wanderings on the road to Golgotha
are in abeyance.
In the daylight, like Breughel's peasants,
they will resume being lost.

That Red Stuff

... When Jacob had cooked stew, Esau came in from the field and he was famished; and Esau said to Jacob, "Please let me have a swallow of that red stuff there, for I am famished"... But Jacob said, "First sell me your birthright."
Genesis 25:29-34

What fine stew that must have been,
what aroma to whet that biblical appetite,
what lentils
to warrant so steep a price
which even Jack would not have paid.

What brother would have exacted
such a price from his sweating brother
fresh from the field, with the smell of the cows
still upon him
demanding that it be tendered before
a drop of stew could pass his lips.

What would Esau have foresaken,
or Jacob have demanded,
for a warm bowl of borscht
with a nice piece of black bread and sweet butter?
For a plate of kasha varnishkas with simmered onions,
he might have given up the holy sites
and spared us all this bloodshed.

My Month

My calendar says that February is African-American history month, and that's great 'cause every oppressed minority should get at least one month, to make up for all the shit they got dealt in the other eleven, but all I want to know is when is my –

> my mom is Portorican, except she pronounces it Pwerto Reekan, with the "r's" rolled slowly, like dice or her hips, the way Rita Moreno did in that song when she danced, with her fuck you attitude and her fuck me stance, and my abuelo was part Cubano, except my mom pronounces it bastard, 'cause he left my abuelita when she was still pregnant, and my dad, who also split on account of pregnancy, must have been Black 'cause I have this great caramel skin which I didn't get from laying out in the sun or spray-on tan, and he had one helluva' laugh, which I never got to hear first-hand and one mean right hook which my mom never saw coming before he left, and now I share my bed and my heart with a pierced, pale-skinned girl from Russia with a great accent and small tits (like a boy, she says) whose mom and dad don't know she's a dyke 'cause she don't feel like explaining it and they wouldn't understand anyway, and they think she's shacked up in Greenpoint with some guy, and what they don't know won't hurt them –

month.

When do I get my month? Hunh?

Leftovers (for Annie)

The embalmer's art is largely wasted
as good as it was.
It plays now only to an audience which will never appreciate
the work it took.

The subject too -
though thankful for the effort
and complimentary at the result -
doubtless would have disapproved the expense,
which, she would have pointed out
loudly and often,
could have been better spent
on the living.

I can hear her now,
all 4'11" of her,
her cheeks freshly rouged and hair perma-frosted
for eternity
aghast at the make-up
and, worse, the cost
marveling at the platters of freshly-cut finger sandwiches and
crudités
and the lines of well-meaning, but well-fed, mourners
politely, but firmly, inquiring
> as she pockets a cookie or two,
> maybe three, especially those
> chocolatedippedoneswithsprinklesand
> raspberryfilling
> which she could never resist

whether she could wrap those up
for her "guests" waiting downstairs
in the other sanctuary.

The Long Courtship & Short Marriage of Ethel & Ernie[16]

One wonders at the rituals of courtship
      following the many trips each had taken
      down the aisle
      so that both knew by heart
      the path leading toward, and away from,
      the altar
the passionate or tender words
whispered softly
across a football field.

One wonders too at the all too brief union
of these titans
      shorter than, but as turbulent as,
      the coupling of Leda and the swan
      which left both unsatisfied
and imagines that
it was doomed at the moment of ecstasis
when Ernie realized it was either his passion
or his hearing
which must suffer.

As an actor,
he had little choice.

---

16 *Following a year long courtship, Ethel Merman and Ernest Borgnine were married on June 27, 1964. They were divorced on July 28, 1964.*

And Now, For My Next Trick

When the rabbit ears and Zenith allowed,
I would watch in 15" black and white awe
as Elizabeth Montgomery and Barbara Eden
      possessed of powers beyond my
      pre-adolescent comprehension
used their god-like skills
to vacuum their respective living rooms
effortlessly.

Later, on the rare Saturday morning,
      when I was allowed through feigned illness
      to dodge temple,
I would watch as Clark
still in mortal garb
removed his hat and horn-rimmed glasses
      but never his tie or smirk
and trained his laser vision
      capable of burning holes through mountains
on pancakes.

As I hear the tale
of the transformation of water into wine
and the extraction of water from a rock,
I wonder how it is that such divine skills are used
for such parlor tricks.

As though Moses sought to persuade Pharaoh to release his
enslaved people
by asking him to pick a card,
any card.
And Pharaoh would be left slack-jawed in wonder
as Moses produced the four of spades from his robe.
And yes, that was the card he had chosen.

How did he know?
He must be god's true messenger.
Of course, the children of Israel would be set free.
But first,
do one more.

Yes, very impressive.
Nice trick with the wine.
How about, next time,
ending thirst.

The Stroke

I remember the pull of my father's face
as though gravity had casually exerted its force
only on the left side
and left the right
alone.

As an artist against a canvas
an oarsman against the waves
a violinist against strands of horse hair
but this stroke produced
no image
no motion
no music
only a gurgled scream, comical look and
docile left hand
which, try as it might, could not come to the aid
of the right.

I recall too the sound which emerged from
half his mouth
    which began as words
    but ended as grunts
    with vowels
as they wheeled him out
and I squeezed his working hand and told the half that could
still hear
that he would be well
which he half-believed.

Later, the stroke of the wiper blades
beat time
steadily
rhythmically
with both left and right working.

The Fourth Day

On the third day, when the centurions had returned tired and
drunk to their barracks
and the boulder was moved,
he came out tired and hungry
the wounds healed
the hands and feet no longer porous.

And nothing had changed.
Nothing!
After the whipping which hurt like hell,
and the betrayal of friends
which hurt more.
And the thorns pressed into his skull's thin flesh,
and the blood stinging his eyes.
And the nails hammered through flesh and muscle
into bone,
which he could hear shattering.
And he forgave them,
even the executioner whose sweat and
drunken breath
he could still smell.
He forgave them all.

And the bastards were still at it like before,
only worse,
as though he had never come
or returned.
The Madoffs and Ponzis still in the temple with the other
hustlers
making cold calls
hawking their wares
fleecing the flock.

And the opportunistic louts
who were already lining up to sell trinkets,
souvenirs of his murder -
a thumb here, a splintered sliver of thigh there
from who the hell knows what animal.

Worse yet, the midnight missionaries and
early morning holy rollers
the sanctimonious sons of Caiaphas
      the Falwells, the Robertsons, the Swaggarts
      (he could never keep them straight)
who claimed to know and love him and invoked his name to
commit or excuse
the worst crimes
which made even his thorn-etched skin crawl.

"I was tortured, felt my bones pierced
for these unrepentant shits?
You forsook me to die slowly
for the likes of them?"

Disgusted, he did not overturn any more tables.
Could not be bothered,
too damned tired.

"Enough," he declared,
not caring if his father heard this time.
So, after a good night's sleep and some food,
washed down with a Lacryma Christi,
he did what any self-respecting apostle would have done
and headed off to Mecca.

The Wardrobe

When he decided against all entreaties
to leave the role
for which he had carefully auditioned
and performed to generally good reviews,
      though he would never be as acclaimed as
      his predecessor who could really deliver
      the lines,
      even with that accent
he asked the stage manager
if he could keep some accoutrements,
a few pieces from the wardrobe.

The request was eminently reasonable,
but politely declined.

No, he was told.
They would need the pieces for the new actor
who was still auditioning.

So, the red shoes
and miter would have to stay.
The lily white conscience -
tarnished only by an
ever so brief stint
in the Hitler youth -
he was free to take with him.

Hah Lachma[17]

This is the bread of affliction
which we scarfed down in Fair Lawn, New Jersey
two or three exits past the Marcal factory
our paper landmark on our exodus from Manhattan
into the land of milk and honey
and raised ranches.

This is the salt water into which we dipped
our annual fresh parsley
or boiled potatoes or
hard-boiled eggs
      as we were chastened not to "fill up" on potatoes or
      eggs
for the tears shed by our ancestors
when they cried out in Egypt,
except our ancestors –
those who were not slaughtered in pogroms
before they could cry out -
came from villages far beyond the Nile.

This is the roasted shank bone
of a goat or paschal lamb,
which was really the incinerated drumstick
of the chicken who nobly offered his other bones
for the soup.

---

17 *This is the bread (Aramaic).*

These are the knaidlich - dumplings -
rolled slowly in the palm
with a pinch of freshly-grated ginger
and some parsley saved from the tears
each bearing my aunt's gentle thumbprint.

These are the Maxwell House Haggadahs
stained with drops of sweet red wine
shed by index finger for each plague
as we furtively licked our finger tips
savoring the sweet taste of
frogs, vermin and locusts.

This is the cup for Elijah
carefully poured
as we opened the screen door and invited this
suburban prophet to drink
    but never eat
with us
    just before he poured out his wrath upon
    the nations that devoured Jacob and laid waste his
    dwelling places
careful not to raise our voices
too loud for the gentile neighbors.

This is the family now gone or dispersed.
These are our voices which still echo from the
diaspora of the downstairs rec room.
And these the hard-boiled memories which,
like matzah,
go down hard and swell with time.

A Song for Goldberg

a tune, beginning with theme in ¾
itself a variation
which the 14 year old Goldberg was compelled to play at
night
in cramped quarters, barely room for the keyboard
a soporific for an insomniac
who had no idea what notes fell
on his restless carcass.

a tune, now etched in his marker
which - to the fury of the Columbia engineers -
Glenn hummed and grunted
as he pounded it out furiously
and too fast
in two recordings
separated by years
and contemplated illnesses
until the real thing came along.

a tune, which Daniel performs
much slower than Glenn
more de   li   be   rate
his eyes closed
perhaps contemplating his wife Jacqueline
gone before 43
as notes pile up
then disperse
like traffic at a once congested intersection.
a tune to which I listen after midnight
when my own insomnia teases like a wet dream
and contemplative ghosts come out
to play.

By Your Leave

I take my leave of you
as though there were something left to take.
A plug to be pulled, to send the soiled water home.
A scab to be picked at slowly,
in the hope the wound has ceased to bleed.
A tablecloth to be laundered, so that one cannot tell where the wine once spilled.

Of course, no leave can be taken.
You are not here, having died 27 years ago this May
your memory heralding the arrival of summer
as sure and as potent as my annual gin and tonic.
But leave demands to be taken by those left behind
to send ghosts safely on their way.

Tonight, I will offer Kaddish for your yahrzeit -
an anniversary only one of us can observe -
lighting a candle as we did for your birthday
but one you cannot extinguish
and one on which neither of us can make a wish.

It is said that the soul of the departed rises higher
each time the prayer is said.
Mine remains clad in clay and utterly
earthbound.

The Evangelist

A man appeared on my TV last night
decomposing himself, climbing through
twisted wires which snake around the base of the lamp
dodging the cat
    which - like a cabbie in rush hour traffic –
    regards everything as provocation.
then reappearing on my 27" flat screen.

After managing this miraculous feat,
he appeared with gleaming teeth,
offering to get my tarnished soul
whiter than white
to remove the calcium, lime and rust
from my once clean claw-foot tub of a conscience
with no nasty residue or soap scum.

I did not pay heed to his words
distracted as I was by his mink-like hair
which seemed to wish nothing more than to return safely to
the burrow from which it came
before its mother, sure to be concerned,
noticed it was missing.

I was distracted too by his warnings
delivered with the certainty and precision of
one who had been there
of the flames of damnation which would burn
if I declined his one-time offer.

I sent him on his way with a universal remote
sure that, although he professed to have a
corner on the market
all he had
all he has
all he will ever have
is a market on the corner.

Wachet Auf[18]

There are those who insist, brag even
as though it were an accomplishment of some renown
that they can remember their dreams
in microscopic detail
the smell of toast burning
the sweetness of fresh strawberry preserves
which linger only in their mind's nostrils
or the tongue of their memory.

They will describe the temperature of the waves in which they
drowned before awaking on dry land,
or the scent of their lover's skin
before she de-materialized.

I politely listen, smile even
if the recounted dream warrants or the narrator expects it,
but demur when asked to reciprocate this
show and tell
as this skill eludes me.

I have hard enough time trying to forget
the real nightmares
to record
the fictitious ones.

---

18 *Sleepers wake (German)*.

Time Out (for Pablo)

Forensic experts in Chile have exhumed the remains of the poet, Pablo Neruda.... The Chilean authorities want to establish whether he died of cancer or was poisoned on the orders of Chile's military ruler, Gen. Augusto Pinochet.
     BBC News, 8 April 2013

Sí, por favor exhumen mis huesos.[19]
I tire of this cloistered space
where I have overstayed my welcome
where the ocean's breezes and the scent of my beloved
though tantalizingly close
do not reach,
where the vista so finite and cuisine so limited
and fresh paper and typewriter ribbon
so hard to come by.

Sí, por favor exhumen mis huesos.
I do not wish to share the same earth as Augusto
with his trimmed moustache and crisp uniform.
Though he has moved to more southern climes
far more tropical than here,
his stench still fouls up the place.

Sí, por favor exhumen mis huesos,
if only to cause sleepless nights
for the little general and his accomplices
who, though lacking hands,
still have blood on them
from the thousands of mis compatriotas,
now mis vecinos.

---

19 *Yes, please exhume my bones.*

Sí, por favor exhumen mis huesos.
I cannot say what tale they will tell
    dispatched like Hamlet's father
    or a more prosaic finale.
A writer never reveals his ending.
It is a voyage of discovery
upon which we will embark together.

But first,
take me outside.
I long to feel the sun on my tired bones.

Marathon

Doubtless, Philippides had no time to wash the stain and
stench
of battle, before he ran
fresh from the carnage of Marathon.

His sandals still caked with blood and viscera
of defeated Persians
or victorious Athenians.
Sandals are neutral.
Like the Swiss, they do not distinguish between victor and
vanquished.
Yet seem to wind up only on the former's side.

History does not record whether
he loaded up on carbs before he ran
or stretched.
Perhaps, he should have stretched.

No onlookers cheered or offered water
in the searing August heat.
We do not even know his age
or whether parents, or wife,
or young child,
waited to greet him
or saw him cross the finish line.

We know only that he exclaimed "νενικηκαμεν"[20]
and then, in glorious victory, died
ending the race a triumphant
corpse.

---

20 *Pronounced nenikekamen, meaning "We won".*

This race has a bloody past.
No less dipped in turmoil
than tea in water,
leaving both forever changed.
So, this latest carnage came as no surprise.

I no longer marvel at our infinite capacity
for cruelty,
inventing ever more resourceful means of separating
limbs from their owners.

And then,
I saw the photo of another bloody Philippides
his race-worn legs left behind him
carried in the arms of a firefighter
across a different finish line
and exclaimed "νενικηκαμεν".
We won.

Strawberries

The strawberries do not put up much of a fight
as I make my incision
and smoothly cut away the offending stem.
They do not struggle
or squirm
or even wince in anticipatory pain.

There is some strawberry blood
spilled
but it is sweet
and does not detract from the overall smoothness of the
operation.

I was not there when they sliced into you
the first time
to remove a growth then
no larger than a strawberry.
It could not have been so smooth.
The scar silently bears witness to that.

Afterwards, though, you were as forgiving
and sweet
as the berries which,
like you,
calmly await the knife's next blow.

Wisdom's Gate

At the gates of wisdom
or her intercom, I stand
in the freezing cold, no less
a fool
pressing this buzzer
seeking admission
like Tamino demanding to see Pamina
only to be rebuffed.

Of course, there is no answer.
Why should there be?
For wisdom, no trifling buzzer should suffice
and wisdom wisely
is not at home.

There should be a gong the size of the stadium
in which the refugees from Katrina gathered,
which would resound in the farthest corner
of Tibet.

So that, in some quiet village just now waking up
with animals waiting impatiently to be fed
and children begging for a few more precious minutes of
sleep
a farmer might hear and know
to open the door
and let this fool in.

Memorial Day (2012)

The few old men with vision dim
and vague recall of battles grim.
The children stand in brutal heat
with anxious hands, impatient feet.

The men now sit in vintage cars
with quick salutes and faded stars.
The children wait for music's start
with steps rehearsed til' known by heart.

The few who fought the last good war
too frail to march, too weak by far.
The children blind to war's true cost
of severed legs and brothers lost.

These old men could tell a tale
of wounds grotesque and bodies pale.
But today is one for flags and bands
and who am I to countermand

the joyous sounds of fife and drum.
But something here leaves me numb.
The men too quick to drive away
will tell no tales of limbs astray.
The children now so overjoyed
will hear no tales of lives destroyed.

So children march and scream with glee
and sing hosannas to all that's free.
And old men will offer thanks
they ride in cars, and not in tanks.

If these men could command the ears
of these young children free from fear,
would they praise war without surcease
or would they offer solemn hymns to peace.

Memorial Day (2013)

At the parade, watching
from the granite steps of the Episcopal Church,
I scan the crowds searching for
veterans of the great
and less than great wars.

Barely a handful can be found
amidst the sea of baton twirlers
tugging at their ill-fitting uniforms
and beaming scouts - cub, eagle and girl
    merit badges adorning slender chests
and horn and woodwind players
        essaying only two of Holst's Planets
        Mars, the bringer of war
        and Jupiter, with its solemn hymn.

One wizened warrior from the Great War,
his marching long past, is helped
to sing the anthem and, with that done,
to return home.
His translucent hands and filmy eyes
mistake me for someone else.
Only a few GI Joes, well beyond their
action figure days,
and no doughboys from our wars of this slender century
which rage unseen.

I seek out these soldiers where I know they will be hiding,
two blocks off the parade route,
a safe distance from the bands, batons and balloons.

There, beneath the locust trees
by the cool slabs of marble
I quietly offer and they silently accept
my thanks.

Acknowledgments

Writing has been described as a solitary activity. Perhaps it is so. But, poets and writers – no less than other mortals -- depend upon human interaction for support, sustenance, comfort and (often) material. As the foregoing poems attest, I have depended upon – and am profoundly grateful for -- such interaction and support.

The following people have provided support in a myriad of ways - friendship, inspiration, encouragement or physical and moral support - which has made the writing of these poems (and so much else) possible. Most are living; sadly, some are not. The former are thanked (profusely); the latter are missed (also profusely).

Denise Abercrombie; Duane Andrews; Valerie G. Annis; Mark Ast; Bianca, George & Rares Barbu; Dr. Ed Berman; John Bolster; Ronald Cohen; Ruth Saltzman Deutsch; Sandra Bishop Ebner; Christopher Ellis; Robin Frome; Rev. Jack Gilpin; Arthur Gluckman; Bill Greenman; Susan Grisell; Rabbi Jon Haddon; Bill Huntington; Margaret Kistinger; Terri Klein; Ann Lathrop; Don Lowe; Lisa Martin; Jack McCarthy; Frank McCourt; Marianela Medrano; Gregory Mertl; Nicholas Vincent Miele; Harry Minot; Beverly & Andrew Monthie; Gregory James Mullen; Ralph Nazareth; Marilyn Nelson; Eli Noam; Annie Orr; Oscar Rasmussen; Dimitri Rimsky; Kate Rushin; Dr. Rocco Russo; David Selwyn; Karen Silk; Dr. John Spera; Nadine Strossen; Ron Suresha; Ilene Sussman; Elizabeth Thomas; Sally Tornow; Susan Tuz; Davyne Verstandig; Faith Vicinanza; Mar Walker; Sarah Zimmermann; and – of course -- my brothers (Steven & Mark); my parents (Morton & Anita); and my children (Max & Zoe).

Neil Silberblatt
July 2013

Biography

Neil Silberblatt was born and grew up in New York City and now resides in Connecticut. He has been writing poetry since his college days. His poems have been published in several literary journals including *Verse Wisconsin, Hennen's Observer* and *Naugatuck River Review*. The first collection of Neil's poems – *So Far, So Good* – was published in June 2012 by lulu.com. One of his poems — *Madison Avenue* (included in this collection) — was nominated by *Hennen's Observer* for a Pushcart Prize. Neil has organized a series of poetry readings at venues throughout Connecticut, including The Sherman Playhouse, Minor Memorial Library in Roxbury, Gunn Memorial Library in Washington, Wooster School in Danbury, The Aldrich Contemporary Art Museum in Ridgefield, Hartford Public Library, and the New Britain Museum of American Art. He has been a featured poet at the Confluencia literary reading series at Naugatuck Valley Community College in Waterbury, CT; at the Wednesday Night Poetry Series in Bethel, CT; and at Curley's Diner, a weekly gathering spot for poets and writers in Stamford, CT.

Would you like to see your manuscript become a book?

If you are interested in becoming a PublishAmerica author, please submit your manuscript for possible publication to us at:

acquisitions@publishamerica.com

You may also mail in your manuscript to:

**PublishAmerica
PO Box 151
Frederick, MD 21705**

We also offer free graphics for Children's Picture Books!

www.publishamerica.com

PublishAmerica